INTERNATIONAL FOOTBALL ILLUSTRATED ANNUAL

A vivid all-photographic presentation of your Top Stars and Outstanding Personalities. All the excitement and action of Soccer captured in Brilliant Pictures, Portrait Souvenirs and Superb Team Groups. Packed with photos and facts INTERNATIONAL FOOTBALL ILLUSTRATED ANNUAL is a memorable record of Soccer as it happens.

Copyright © MCMLXX
by Plant News Limited

All rights reserved throughout the world

Published in Great Britain by
WORLD DISTRIBUTORS (Manchester) LIMITED
P.O. Box 111, 12 Lever Street, Manchester M60 1TS

Printed and bound in England by
Jarrold and Sons Ltd, Norwich

SBN 7235 0049 5

ALLAN CLARKE *Cup Final Winner and Loser*

One of the newest of all football's many trophies — "The Man of the Match Award" was instituted in 1969 for presentation to the most outstanding player in the F.A. Cup Final, chosen by the dozens of Soccer reporters in the Wembley Press box. The first winner of this wonderful trophy, worth £500, was Allan Clarke, Leicester City's inside-left, who made such a great impression in his team's magnificent struggle against Manchester City. No man did more to earn a winner's gold medal — but this honour was denied him. A few months after receiving his award from Manager Frank O'Farrell, Allan was transferred to Leeds United for a fee of £165,000 and is now adding to his previous triumphs.

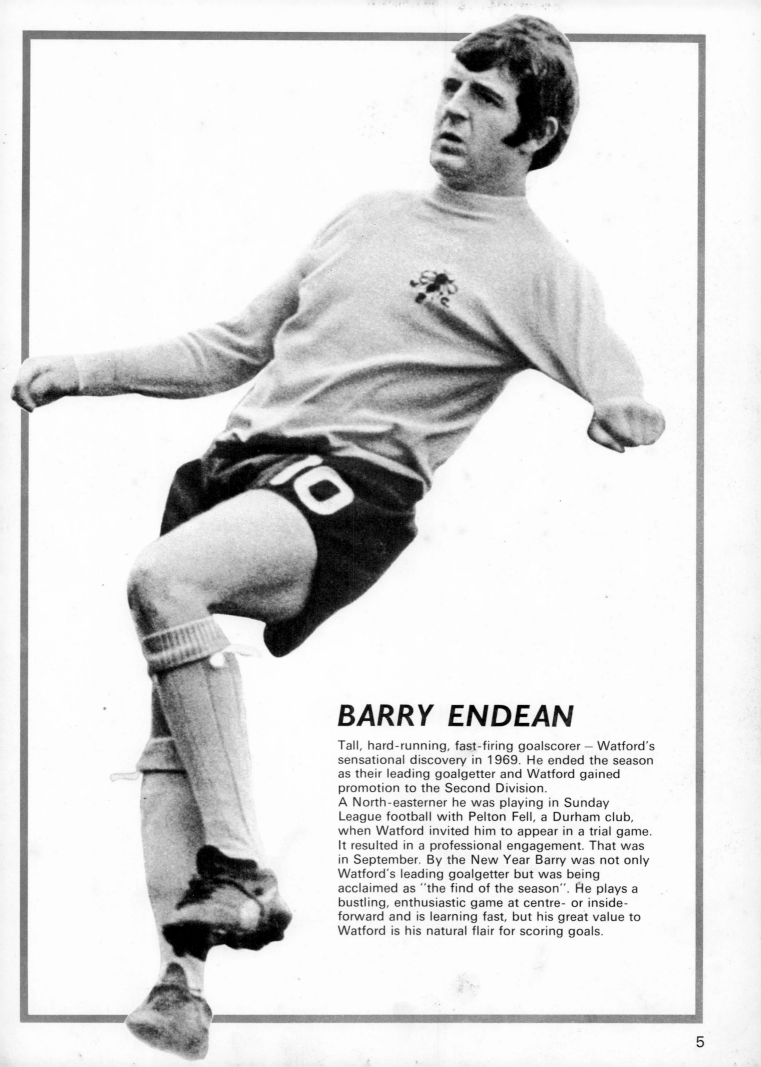

BARRY ENDEAN

Tall, hard-running, fast-firing goalscorer — Watford's sensational discovery in 1969. He ended the season as their leading goalgetter and Watford gained promotion to the Second Division.

A North-easterner he was playing in Sunday League football with Pelton Fell, a Durham club, when Watford invited him to appear in a trial game. It resulted in a professional engagement. That was in September. By the New Year Barry was not only Watford's leading goalgetter but was being acclaimed as "the find of the season". He plays a bustling, enthusiastic game at centre- or inside-forward and is learning fast, but his great value to Watford is his natural flair for scoring goals.

IAN GIBSON

The diminutive goal-maker of Coventry City started his career as a wee winger in Scottish junior football.

He was signed by the now defunct Accrington Stanley and made his League debut at the age of 16.

In 1959 he moved to Bradford, switched to inside-forward, and developed so quickly into a skilful, scheming midfield man that he was transferred to Middlesbrough in March 1962 for £20,000.

He was given the captaincy of the Ayresome Park club and gained a Scottish Under-23 cap. In July 1966 Coventry City secured his transfer for a fee of £60,000, a record for both clubs.

TONY BROWN

He's worth double pay to West Bromwich Albion for Tony is a wing-half and goalscorer rolled into one. Born in Oldham he played his boyhood football as a Manchester schoolboy before joining Albion as an apprentice. He was then a fast, adventurous winger always looking for the goal-chance. He appeared in his first League game in September 1963, three days before he was signed as a full professional. He won an England Youth cap and in 1965—66 was Albion's leading goalgetter — from outside-right. Later he switched to wing-half but has never lost his flair for goals. He has collected a total of more than 80 in the last four seasons, including four during his team's victorious drive to Wembley for the 1968 Final. Most of his goals are "winners".

ALFREDO DI STEFANO

The greatest centre-forward in the history of European football whose name will become a legend, particularly in Spain where he played his finest football. From the moment he stepped on to the field he was in full command, dictating the tempo of the play and overshadowing friend and foe with his quietly efficient personality allied to consummate confidence and skill. Born in Buenos Aires his career began with River Plate Juniors.

In 1946 he shot to fame when he became the club's leading scorer and played for Argentina. Later he moved to Millionarios, Colombia, continued his goalscoring and gained international honours for his adopted country. In 1953 he left South America for Spain, joining Real Madrid for a £24,000 fee. It was a ridiculous fee for the man who was to become the most illustrious player in Europe. His honours with Real are well known — five European Cup triumphs in successive seasons (1956–60); at least one goal in each of those Finals; dozens of caps for Spain; every possible Spanish League and Cup honour, and the honour of captaining the Rest of the World XI against England at Wembley in 1963.

He ended his fantastic career with two seasons at Espanol Barcelona and retired in 1966 at the age of 39. He was truly world famous and his name will never be forgotten, for Alfredo di Stefano was as grand a sportsman, in every aspect, as he was a master with a football.

Star

SIR ALF RAMSEY

It is often forgotten that the man whose planning and inspiration as manager and mentor of England's international football teams had so much to do with the winning of the World Cup was once a very great player himself. Born at Dagenham, in Essex, he was playing in Army football during the war when he was invited to join Southampton as a full-back. When the war ended, Alf Ramsey, as he was then, began his rise to fame and in 1949 was transferred to Tottenham Hotspur, after making his debut in the England team. He ended his playing career in 1955 with 32 caps and Division 1 and 2 Championship medals won with the Spurs. He was a classic type of full-back.

In August 1955 he became manager of Ipswich Town, and was instrumental in building a team that won the Second and First Division Championships in successive seasons. He took over the managerial role of England's international teams in 1963, with the result that is too well known to need detailed elaboration. He was knighted in 1966 for his services to football — and more particularly the success of his World Cup team.

# of Yesterday

JIM McCALLIOG

Jim McCalliog was one of the top transfers of the 1969 close season when he moved from Sheffield Wednesday to the Wolves for a £70,000 fee. Jim, seen here in action against Peter Dobing, of Stoke City, has all the natural Scottish flair for the game he plays so well in any forward position, as striker or midfield schemer. Glasgow-born he joined Chelsea as an unknown lad but made rapid progress. After only seven first-team games, however, he was transferred to Sheffield Wednesday for a fee of £37,500. It seemed a ridiculous fee for a lad of so little experience but the Yorkshire club knew what they were doing. He rose to Scottish international rank, became a power in the Wednesday attack and scored a brilliant goal in the 1966 Cup Final. Then, after 150 League games in four seasons he was transferred to Wolves where he quickly established himself.

*Manchester City's
"Goal"den Boy*

NEIL YOUNG

One goal was sufficient to win the F.A. Cup in April 1969 — but what a glorious goal it was. In the twenty-third minute of the first half Manchester City's Mike Summerbee raced through the Leicester City defence and from the by-line put across a perfect centre that dropped about 15 yards from the goal. Inside-left Neil Young, standing unmarked, hit the ball first time with his lethal left foot. It screamed into the top of the net, despite the desperate leap of young Peter Shilton. It was indeed a golden goal, scored by a player who has the respect of all opponents — particularly the goalkeepers — because of his flair for snapping up chances.

Born in Manchester he joined the City club as a slim 15-year-old apprentice in 1960 — two days before Manchester United sought his signature! Since then tall, hefty Neil has appeared in nearly 300 first team games and scored dozens of goals — but none that gave him greater satisfaction than his Wembley Cup-winner!

JOHN McGRATH

Tall, powerfully built pivot around whom the Southampton defence revolves. A centre-half of wide experience. Manchester-born he had trials with Bolton Wanderers but was allowed to join the junior staff at Bury. He stepped into the League side in 1957, played in nearly 150 games before his transfer to Newcastle United in 1961, and remained at St. James's Park for seven years. During that period he appeared in another 120 League games and then left for Southampton in February 1968 for a £30,000 fee. John, who gained an England Under-23 cap in 1961, has proved a tower of strength to the Saints.

PETER STOREY

Arsenal introduced him to First Division football during the 1965–66 season and he has never looked back. The sturdy young full-back with rugged determination, resolute in his tackling and menacing in his attacking runs from deep defence, has now played in nearly 200 first-team games for the Gunners.

A native of Farnham, Hampshire, he learned his football as an Aldershot schoolboy and in 1961 won his England Schools cap in the same side as Johnny Sissons (West Ham) and Glyn Pardoe (Manchester City). He became an Arsenal apprentice straight from school and has made rapid progress to stardom.

Always good pals off the field but let them meet on it –

BROTHERS

There is no need to identify these two famous members of an honoured football family. The Charlton brothers have risen to the heights of fame since both set out as boys from their Ashington, Northumberland, home to tread the football trail, Jackie, the elder, with Leeds United and Bobby with Manchester United. For some years their only meetings on the football field were as opponents for they had never played together in the same team until Jackie was chosen to join Bobby in the England team against Scotland in 1965. Their alliance has been repeated many times since then, including the World Cup Final of 1966. But at least twice each season the two Charltons meet as opponents in League matches between Leeds United and Manchester United — close rivals, too, for as you know Jackie is a close-marking centre-half and Bobby, usually at centre-forward, comes in for careful attention from "big brother". On such occasions family relationships are completely forgotten in the grim battle for League points.

Bobby has admitted that Jackie is one of the hardest opponents he has to face, while Jackie is loud in his praises of Bobby's ability to beat anyone on two legs. Fortunately for Bobby he is not tall enough to challenge big brother Jackie when the ball is in the air — but then perhaps he doesn't need to!

OPPOSED!

In 1958 a young half-back named Allan Harris, from the Hackney area of East London, was awarded his England Schools cap. That same year, at the age of 15, he joined the Chelsea junior staff.

In 1960 Allan's brother Ron followed the same road to Stamford Bridge following his success as an England schoolboy. Allan was first to gain senior team status, but Ron soon joined his brother and over the next two seasons they often appeared as team-mates. On several occasions they played for Chelsea as partners at full-back. Then came the family parting, when Allan was transferred to Coventry City in November 1964. But after 18 months he returned to Chelsea.

So the brothers were reunited and Allan was a member of Chelsea's 1967 Cup Final team captained by Ron. Two months later Allan moved again, this time to Queen's Park Rangers, then in Division 3. But the Rangers shot up into the First Division in two years and the Harris brothers became opponents for the first time in their careers. In September 1968 Queen's Park Rangers met Chelsea and the two sides were skippered by the Harris brothers. (Picture above.) Unfortunately Allan and Ron have now drifted apart once more for Queen's Park Rangers are back in Division 2.

FRANCISCO GENTO

Real Madrid

One of the most popular left-wingers in Europe and star of Real Madrid since 1953. Gento (pronounced Hento) holds a record that may not be beaten for many years — if at all.

Since 1956 Real have appeared in eight European Cup Finals, and the swarthy little man with rocket propulsion has played in them all, winning six gold medals. A champion sprinter in his youth he took up football with a junior side Nueva Montana, progressed with Astillero and Santander and joined Real in 1953, winning the first of many Spanish caps two years later. He was also a member of the F.I.F.A. side that met England at Wembley in 1963 in the F.A. Centenary match.

Francisco Gento's years of glory on the Soccer stage have almost reached the final curtain, and we may not see him again displaying his arts and his fantastic speed in top-class football, but his name will never be forgotten.

TOMMY LAWRENCE

Liverpool's burly Scottish goalkeeper from Dailly, Ayrshire, has now made over 250 League appearances for the Anfield club since 1962. He joined 'Pool as an amateur in 1956, turning professional after a few months. For six years he remained an understudy but patience was one of his virtues and eventually his big chance came. Since then "Big Tom" has won League Championship and Cup medals and his Scottish international cap, a tribute to his courage and consistency in the Liverpool goal. No man is more deserving of the success for which he waited so patiently and worked so hard to attain.

Made his entry into First Division football in 1968 and has rocketed into prominence with some sterling displays at centre-half and wing-half. Yet before joining Spurs in January 1968 the tall 21-year-old had had no previous first-class experience except with his home town club Chelmsford City in the Southern League.
Spurs secured his transfer for a fee of £5,500 with the promise of a further £3,000 should he appear in ten first-team games. That additional fee had to be paid a few months later. The future looks very promising for Peter Collins.

PETER COLLINS

LEEDS UNITED

left to right: (back row)
Paul Madeley,
Mike O'Grady,
(now with Wolves)

David Harvey,
Gary Sprake,
Jack Charlton,
Norman Hunter,

(centre row)
Albert Johanneson,
Rodney Belfitt,

Mick Jones,
Terry Hibbitt,
Eddie Gray,

Peter Lorimer;
(front row)
Paul Reaney,

Terry Cooper,
Johnny Giles,
Billy Bremner (Captain),

Jimmy Greenhoff
(now with Stoke City)
Michael Bates.

BILLY BREMNER

Few players have made a greater impression on the game in general and on the fans all over Britain — and in Europe — than the little Scots skipper of Leeds United. The wee red-head from Stirling joined Leeds as a junior in 1958, after winning a Scottish Schools cap.

From the beginning it was obvious that he was destined for greatness, and the recent fame of United owes much to his dynamic personality and leadership. He never spares himself on the field, whether he is wearing the white of Leeds or the blue of his native country — and he expects utmost effort from his colleagues.

LEN GLOVER

The Charlton Athletic fans were shocked in November 1967 when they learned that Len Glover, a great favourite at the Valley, had been transferred to Leicester City for a fee of £80,000.

He was born in South-east London, played his schoolboy football there and graduated to stardom through the Charlton Athletic colts and junior sides, finally turning full professional in 1962. He became one of the top wingers in Division 2, fast, skilful and provider of precision passes, and played in more than 200 first-team games before his move to Leicester, where he has enhanced his reputation as a fast-raiding striker.

PETER DOWNS-BOROUGH

In 1961 a tall, slim young goalkeeper made his first appearance in League football with Halifax Town. At that time he was quite unknown — except to his close friends in Halifax, where he was born and reared.

On 15 March 1969 however, Peter Downsborough thrilled 100,000 fans at Wembley with a masterly display of goalkeeping for Swindon Town against Arsenal in the Football League Cup Final. There were times when he alone stood between the rampaging Arsenal attackers and a goal, but Peter's superb performance came as no surprise to those who have followed his career. Although he has missed the game's top honours he has gained a wealth of experience, first with Halifax Town, for whom he played in 148 League games, and since 1965 with the Swindon Robins in another century of matches.

GORDON MARSHALL

Towards the end of the 1968–69 season Hibernian announced the signing of Gordon Marshall from Nottingham Forest. The news caused a stir of excitement in Edinburgh for the big, hefty goalkeeper was well known in the City. It was there that he began his first-class Soccer career with Hearts, Hibs' local rivals. During the early 1960s he was a tower of strength in the Hearts goal and helped to win both the League Championship and League Cup. In 1963 he was transferred to Newcastle United and helped the Magpies to the Second Division Championship.

Then in April 1969, after more than 180 first team games for Newcastle, Gordon was hurriedly transferred to Nottingham Forest to take the place of their injured goalie Peter Grummitt. It was just a temporary move and now he's with Hibernian. Gordon, in spite of his name and his long association with Scotland, was born at Farnham, in Surrey. This was discovered some years ago when he was chosen to play for Scotland in an Under-23 international but reluctantly had to admit that he was not a Scot. His reward was a place in the England Under-23 team AGAINST Scotland!

PHIL PARKES

Wolves' very capable goalkeeper. A six-footer with a dedicated approach to his onerous task he has made remarkable progress during the last two seasons. Phil comes from nearby West Bromwich and made his first impression on the game as a local schoolboy. He joined Wolves' apprentice staff in 1963 and took the full-time professional ticket a year later. In 1966–67 he was given the chance he had long awaited. At the opening of the season he was only fourth-team goalie, but in February had made such progress that he was given the first-team spot and retained it. At the end of that season Wolves won promotion to the First Division.

RODNEY MARSH

When Queen's Park Rangers signed the tall inside-forward from Fulham in March 1966 for a £15,000 fee they secured their ticket to the First Division. His transfer meant him dropping from First to Third Division status, but within two years he had made the return trip, for Queen's Park Rangers climbed from the Third Division to the First in successive seasons (1967 and 1968). They also became the first Third Division club to win the Football League Cup (1967).

Rodney Marsh must be given his full share of credit for this wonderful performance with his excitingly unorthodox and often brilliant work and his fantastic goalscoring. But injury forced him into a long period of inactivity during the 1968–69 season. At the time of his injury Rodney Marsh had played twice for England Under-23 teams and was being considered for Sir Alf Ramsey's senior squad. But last season he regained all his old brilliance and goals flair.

COLIN BELL

DAVID SADLER

Colin Bell (blue shirt) and David Sadler are the best of good friends although they play for different clubs. Colin is the goal-poaching schemer of Manchester City, whom he joined from Bury, while David, an amateur international at 16, has become one of the strong men in the Manchester United defence after his early success as a forward. He was at inside-left when United won the European Cup in 1968, proving his value as an all-rounder. David and Colin both appeared for England in Under-23 and senior internationals during the 1967–68 season. Colin Bell, ''general'' of the City strategy, has since leapt into the top ranks with more caps and League Championship and Cup medals.

RON YEATS

Captain of Liverpool since he joined them in 1962 the big, hefty Scottish centre-half has won the game's highest honours — Championship and Cup medals and Scottish caps. Ron comes from Aberdeen, where he once worked as a slaughterer. He came to prominence as a footballer with Dundee United, playing as a part-timer while doing his National Service in the Army.

He accepted the move to Merseyside and Dundee United banked a fee of £35,000. It was a move that put the big Scot's feet firmly on the ladder that has led to fame and fortune, for Ron, idol of the Spion Kop, is now a successful businessman in Liverpool. He has earned his name with his selfless efforts for the Reds of Anfield and his own dominating personality.

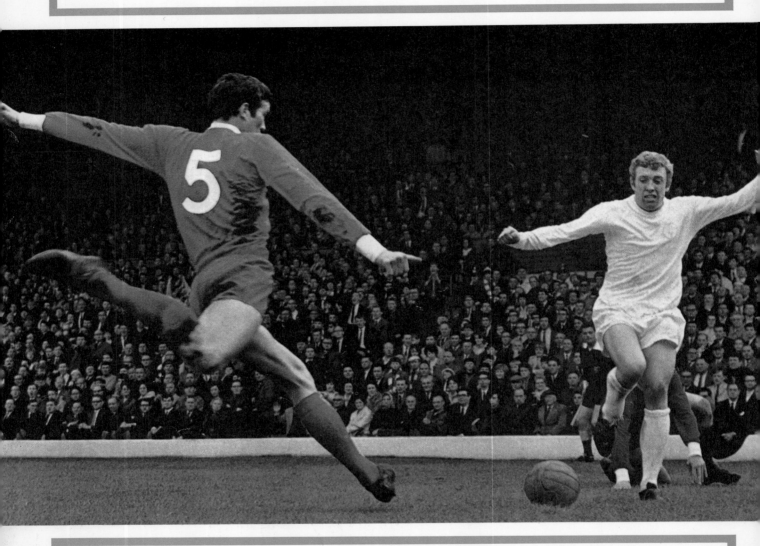

MICK JONES

Tall, skilful centre-forward with a penchant for scoring valuable goals, he cost Leeds United a fee of £100,000 when he joined them from Sheffield United in September 1967. Since then he has become an outstanding Soccer-striker and has played his full part in the romantic rise to fame of the brilliant Leeds side.

A native of Worksop, Mick served his "apprenticeship" with Sheffield United and had played for England at Youth, Under-23 and Senior levels before his costly move to Leeds. During the 1968–69 season he added to his international experience. In this dramatic picture he is challenging Ron Yeats, the big Scots skipper of Liverpool.

ALAN BALL

Everton's flame-haired little dynamo, is aptly nicknamed "Ball of Fire". From kick-off to final whistle he never stops running; believes that there is no maximum to a player's work-rate on the field and no opposition that cannot be beaten. He proved that in the World Cup games of 1966, particularly in that tense Final. Son of the Preston North End manager, Alan was born into Soccer. He achieved early fame with Blackpool and cost Everton a fee of £110,000 in 1966. He stands only 5 ft. 7 in. and was once told he was too small to become a first-class footballer . . . too small!

FRANZ BECKENBAUER

Tall, handsome pin-up idol of West Germany, was only 20 when he played a storming game for his country in the 1966 World Cup Final. A half-back who loves to use his speed to throw panic into opposing defences, he has won top honours with his club Bayern Munich.

Often referred to as the "Bobby Moore of West Germany" he rose to fame through his country's schoolboy and youth teams and earned his first senior international honour in 1965.

During the summer Terry was signed by Hull City as their player-manager. They could not have made a wiser choice; the tall, elegant centre-half who spent 11 seasons with Arsenal is a true professional, dedicated to soccer and a born leader. Since 1960 he has played for Ireland on more than 40 occasions, captaining the side in many of these internationals. He was only 17 when he joined the Gunners from Bangor in 1959 but made rapid progress to stardom.

TERRY NEILL

JOHN TALBUT/JOHN KAYE

The strong man of the West Bromwich Albion defence, good in the air and a resolute tackler. The tall North-easterner is a product of South Shields schools football and captained the England team in 1955. He joined the Burnley junior staff in 1956 and developed into a powerful centre-half, playing in more than 60 League games before his transfer to West Bromwich Albion in December 1966 for £30,000. He helped Albion win the F.A. Cup in 1968 and during the 1963–64 season played seven times for England Under-23 teams, captaining the side.

The player on the left is John Kaye, Albion's powerful midfield link-man, who adopted the position after several seasons as a striker.

THE LATCHFORD BROTHERS

During the 1968–69 season Birmingham City gave their local-born Latchford brothers their first taste of League football — Dave, the elder, in goal, and Bob at centre-forward.

Football has been their life since early boyhood. Both came to prominence in Birmingham Schools teams and both became apprentices at the age of 15 with Birmingham City, Dave signed as a full-time professional in 1966 and Bob in 1968. Both gained England Youth caps and developed together in Birmingham Youth and reserve sides. Six-footer Dave, now aged 21, has proved that he is ready for a first-team place although last season he was mainly understudy to Scotland's 'keeper Jim Herriot. Bob, tall, bounding with energy, hungry for goalscoring chances, could become an outstanding centre-forward for he is still only 19 and with more experience will come maturity. There is a bright future for these Birmingham-born footballing brothers.

Yet a third brother, Peter, a member of the England senior basketball team, is also, like brother Dave, a very promising goalkeeper with professional ambitions. But Peter has joined the junior staff of West Bromwich Albion.

RON HARRIS

The youngest-ever captain of a Cup Final team, Ron was only 22 when he led Chelsea against Spurs in 1967. Born in North-east London he followed his elder brother Allan into the England Schools side (1960) and joined him on the Chelsea junior staff. He played his first games in the senior team at the age of 17 (1962) and has since become one of the most formidable wing-halves in the First Division.

He sets an inspiring example to his colleagues with his fantastic work-rate and super-abundance of fighting spirit. He has gained Youth and Under-23 caps to add to his schoolboy honours and played at left-back when Chelsea won the Football League Cup in 1965. He led Chelsea to victory in last season's F.A. Cup final.

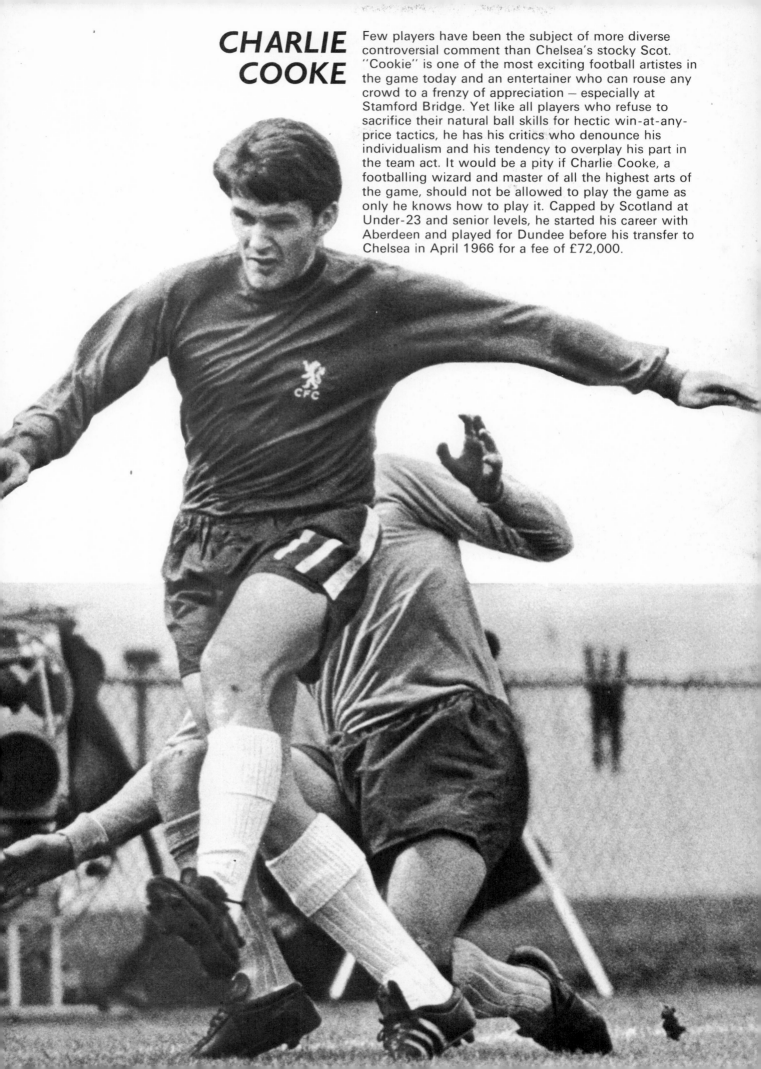

CHARLIE COOKE

Few players have been the subject of more diverse controversial comment than Chelsea's stocky Scot. "Cookie" is one of the most exciting football artistes in the game today and an entertainer who can rouse any crowd to a frenzy of appreciation — especially at Stamford Bridge. Yet like all players who refuse to sacrifice their natural ball skills for hectic win-at-any-price tactics, he has his critics who denounce his individualism and his tendency to overplay his part in the team act. It would be a pity if Charlie Cooke, a footballing wizard and master of all the highest arts of the game, should not be allowed to play the game as only he knows how to play it. Capped by Scotland at Under-23 and senior levels, he started his career with Aberdeen and played for Dundee before his transfer to Chelsea in April 1966 for a fee of £72,000.

Stars of the Past

There was a time when Arsenal were the greatest team in Britain. During the 1930s the Highbury Gunners were League Champions five times in eight seasons and once runners-up, and twice Cup-winners in three Finals. It was a colossal record. Among the many great players who wore Arsenal's red shirt during that history-making period were Cliff Bastin and Ted Drake. Cliff, fair-haired, ruddy-cheeked Devon lad, joined the Gunners from Exeter City at the age of 17. Before he was 21 he had won every honour in the game as a brilliant, goalscoring left-winger. In 1932—33 he created an all-time record by scoring 33 League goals. Before he retired he had won five League Championship medals; two Cup medals and 21 England caps.

CLIFF BASTIN

Ted Drake was another great goalscorer but as a centre-forward. A native of Southampton he played for that club before his transfer to Arsenal in 1933. Fearless to a degree he played in the 1936 Cup Final although still suffering from a bad knee injury and scored the only goal. In December 1935 he set a record when he hit seven goals in a League match — on Aston Villa's ground. He later managed Chelsea and Reading.
Their names will never be forgotten at Highbury.

TED DRAKE

"Farewell and Good Luck Bryan!"

Bryan Douglas is a name that has become famous in the football world — illustrious in Blackburn where the little man was born and has spent all his Soccer life. He joined Blackburn Rovers in 1954 as a tiny inside-forward, so small and frail, in fact, that he was switched to the right-wing. It was a wise move, for Bryan developed into one of the finest wingmen in the game. In 1957 he was first chosen for the England team and from then until 1963 gained 36 international caps, although during the latter years he reverted to his original position at inside-forward. Now, after 15 years with Blackburn Rovers and over 450 League appearances for the club, he has now hung up his football boots. What a pity it is that such great players as Bryan Douglas have to grow older and eventually make their final bow from the Soccer stage. The retirement of Blackburn's brilliantly skilful and much honoured star is a great loss to English football, for not only was he an elegant player, a joy to watch, but his sportsmanship both on and off the field was of the highest order. Players, officials and his thousands of admirers on the terraces will wish him the best of good luck in the future.

In this picture Bryan is recalling some of his memories with his two sons, Stephen and Graham.

JIMMY JOHNSTONE

There's always danger when the red-headed little Celtic winger goes racing into the goal area. He hasn't much weight to throw around but he's always eager to have a go for goal. Jimmy Johnstone, non-stop dynamo, elusive as an eel and resilient as elastic, with terrific courage and determination, is one of the reasons why Celtic lifted Scotland's "triple crown" in 1968—69, and last season added two more trophies to their ever-growing list of honours.

Here's Jimmy challenging the jumping ability of Bobby Reid, Raith Rovers' goalie.

ALAN OAKES

One of the finest wing-halves in the First Division. Quiet and unobtrusive in his play yet his work-rate is tremendous, prompting and scheming in midfield but always ready to lend his height and weight in attack — or defence.

Born at Winsford, Cheshire, he had played only schoolboy football when he joined the junior ranks of Manchester City in 1958 after he had attracted the club's notice as captain of the Cheshire Schools team. In November 1959, aged 17, the tall lad from a country village played his first game in the League side. Since then he has put more than 350 appearances behind him and has earned the title of "Mr. Consistency" among the Maine Road fans. Incidentally, his cousin, Glyn Pardoe, now Alan's Manchester City colleague and England Under-23 star, comes from the same Cheshire village.

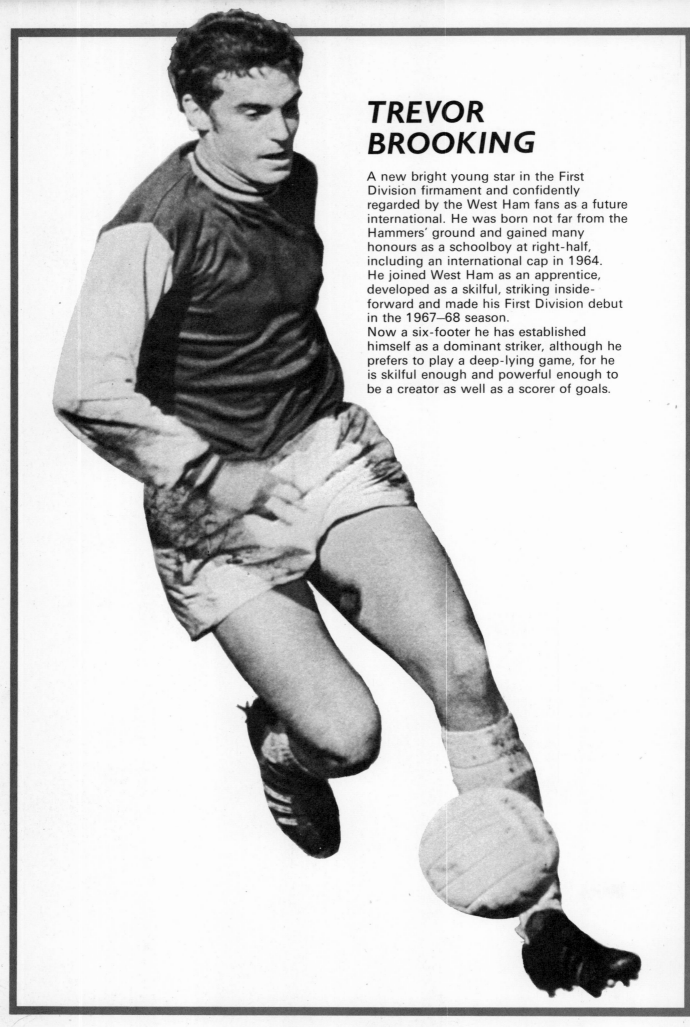

TREVOR BROOKING

A new bright young star in the First Division firmament and confidently regarded by the West Ham fans as a future international. He was born not far from the Hammers' ground and gained many honours as a schoolboy at right-half, including an international cap in 1964. He joined West Ham as an apprentice, developed as a skilful, striking inside-forward and made his First Division debut in the 1967–68 season.

Now a six-footer he has established himself as a dominant striker, although he prefers to play a deep-lying game, for he is skilful enough and powerful enough to be a creator as well as a scorer of goals.

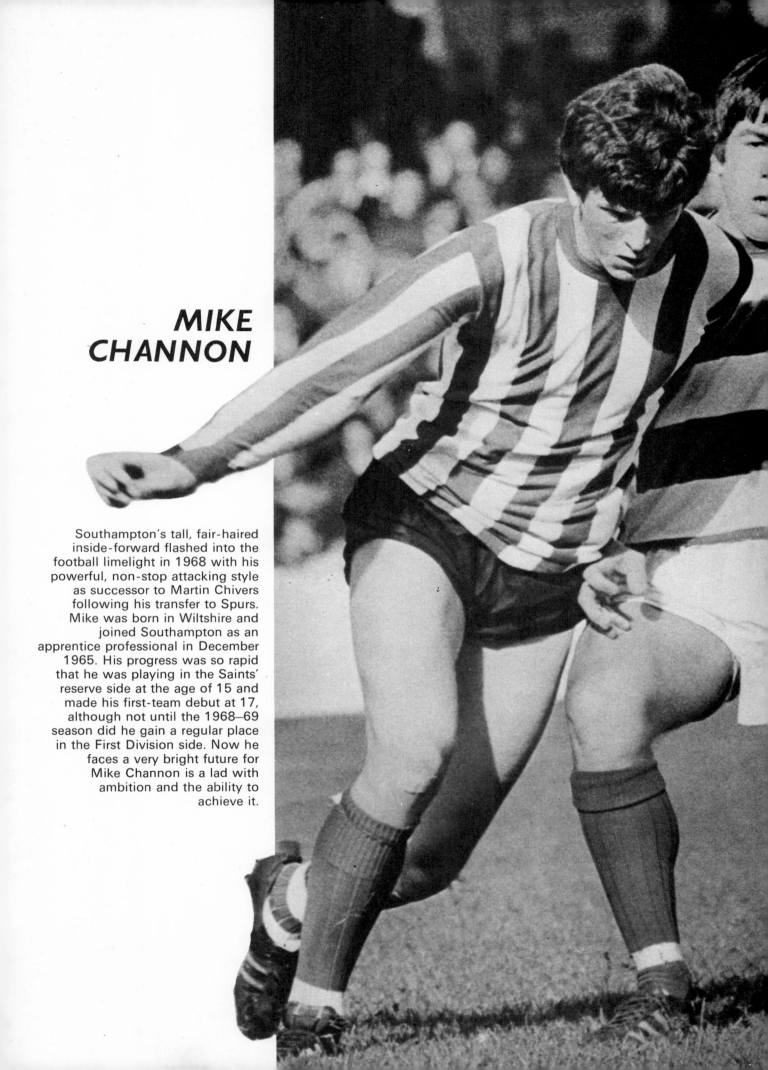

MIKE CHANNON

Southampton's tall, fair-haired inside-forward flashed into the football limelight in 1968 with his powerful, non-stop attacking style as successor to Martin Chivers following his transfer to Spurs. Mike was born in Wiltshire and joined Southampton as an apprentice professional in December 1965. His progress was so rapid that he was playing in the Saints' reserve side at the age of 15 and made his first-team debut at 17, although not until the 1968—69 season did he gain a regular place in the First Division side. Now he faces a very bright future for Mike Channon is a lad with ambition and the ability to achieve it.

Celtic's "Goal"den Boy Bobby Lennox

When Celtic beat Rangers 4—0 in the 1969 Scottish Cup Final, the goal that really clinched the victory was the second. Skipper Billy McNeill shook Rangers with a glorious header after two minutes, but from then until a short time before the interval Celtic were held fast by their Glasgow rivals. Then came the shot that set Hampden Park rocking — a glorious rocket-drive that flashed past Norrie Martin, Rangers' goalie, and hit the back of the net. The man who put it there was that ace-sharpshooter Bobby Lennox, Celtic's Scottish international inside-left. No wonder he cannot disguise his delight as he turns to receive the plaudits of the Parkhead fans and the congratulations of his own team-mates.

It was the first time Celtic had beaten Rangers in the Scottish Cup Final since 1904. Rangers were the winners in 1963 (3—0) and 1966 (1—0). In point of fact it was the first time Rangers had lost a Scottish Cup Final since 1929. But the Celts k.o.'d their Ibrox rivals in the 1966 and 1967 Scottish League Cup Finals — and it was Bobby Lennox who hit the winning goal in the second of those memorable games.

"I've been through it all before", says Tommy Gemmell, Celtic's tall, determined left-back, as he takes a well-earned drink from the Scottish Cup after his team's crushing 4—0 victory over their Glasgow rivals, Rangers, in the 1969 Final. It was Tommy's third Scottish Cup triumph (1965—67—69). Celtic also won the Scottish League Championship and the League Cup that season, which meant that Tommy Gemmell had played a prominent part in his club's honours hat-trick for the second time. The previous occasion was in 1967 when the Celts completed the most fantastic record of all time by becoming the first British club to be crowned "European Champions". Celtic have now taken the lead over Rangers in the Scottish Cup competition — 20 victories against 19 by Rangers. But the Ibrox men still have a lead of nine League Championship successes over Celtic — 34 to 25.

Tommy Gemmell about to take a well-earned sip of champagne from the beribboned Celtic Trophy

PAUL REANEY

Since leaving the Elland Road ground staff to sign as a full professional in October 1961, slim, wiry Paul Reaney has developed into a really fine full-back and a member of one of the finest footballing sides in the country. He was born close to Fulham's ground but his family moved to Leeds and he grew up as a footballer in local schools teams. He has now played in well over 350 first team games for the club; has appeared in F.A. Cup; Inter-Cities Fairs Cup and Football League Cup Finals. During the 1969–70 season he stepped up into the full England side after gaining his Under-23 cap, but a broken leg prevented him joining the World Cup side in Mexico.

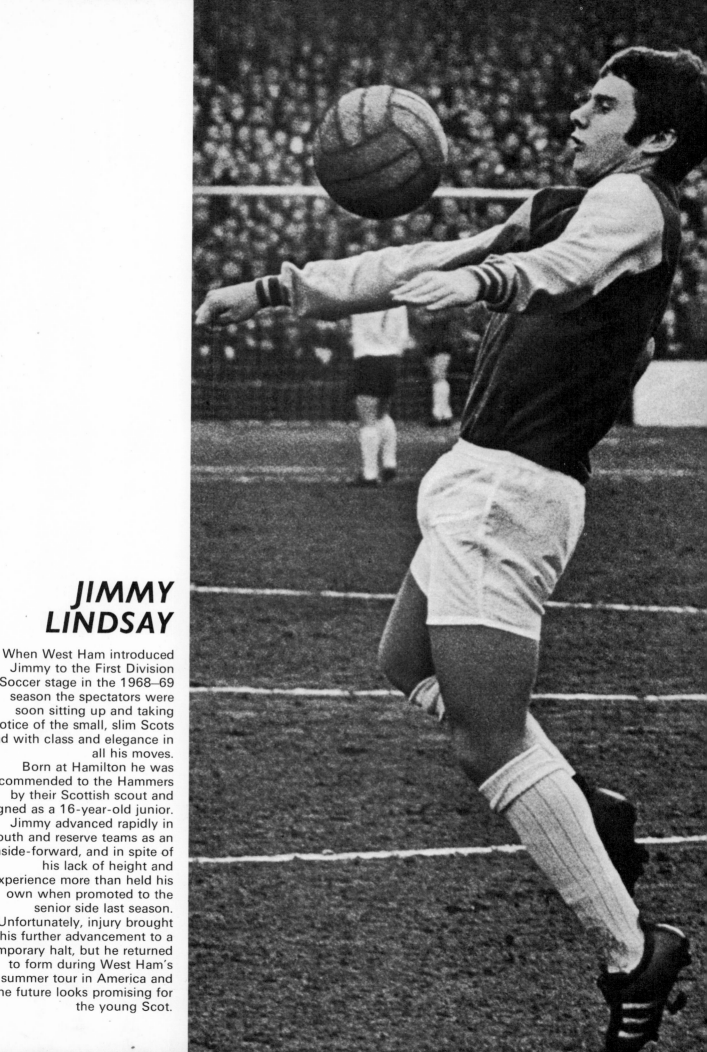

JIMMY LINDSAY

When West Ham introduced Jimmy to the First Division Soccer stage in the 1968—69 season the spectators were soon sitting up and taking notice of the small, slim Scots lad with class and elegance in all his moves.

Born at Hamilton he was recommended to the Hammers by their Scottish scout and signed as a 16-year-old junior.

Jimmy advanced rapidly in Youth and reserve teams as an inside-forward, and in spite of his lack of height and experience more than held his own when promoted to the senior side last season. Unfortunately, injury brought his further advancement to a temporary halt, but he returned to form during West Ham's summer tour in America and the future looks promising for the young Scot.

CHARLIE GEORGE

If ever a lad was born to play for Arsenal it's Charlie George, 19-year-old inside forward and one of the most exciting newcomers to the First Division scene for a long time. Born within earshot of Highbury he was an Arsenal "fan" from the age of three; earned his first Soccer honours as a local schoolboy and achieved his ambition when he became a Highbury apprentice at the age of 15. One of his masters was Bobby Wilson, now Arsenal's star goalie. From his earliest games in the Youth side it was obvious that the tall, slim, fanatical youngster had star potential. Arsenal's famous coach Don Howe spoke of him as possessing the Bobby Charlton touch in midfield and the poaching style of Jimmy Greaves near goal. Young Charlie certainly made a big impression with over 100 goals in the Youth and reserve teams and it came as no surprise when he was given his first-team baptism in the opening game of the 1969–70 season. There was nothing sensational in his debut but his potential was obvious, and in the next match, on the West Bromwich ground, he scored a really fine goal — the match-winner. It would be unfair to the 19-year-old six-footer to praise him too highly but he has natural talent and exuberant enthusiasm, for football means everything to him. With experience will come maturity and stardom.

BOB WILSON

From schoolboy international to First Division. That is the career in brief of Arsenal's popular goalkeeper, but the rise to fame has not been easy for the tall, quiet, genial chap from Chesterfield.

In 1957 Bob Wilson was England Schools goalkeeper. Many of his team-mates in those internationals — Nobby Stiles and Bobby Tambling were among them — joined big clubs as juniors, but he remained at Chesterfield Grammar School and later went to Loughborough College. He played as an amateur for Wolves who offered him professional terms, but he turned them down. In 1963 he took a teaching post in London and agreed to join Arsenal as an amateur. A year later he turned professional, but not until towards the end of the 1967–68 season did he clinch a permanent place in Arsenal's first team. In fact, during his first four years at Highbury he played in only nine League games. Yet he never lost heart and today his persistent patience has been rewarded, for Bob Wilson is now one of the top 'keepers in the First Division.

LEV YASHIN

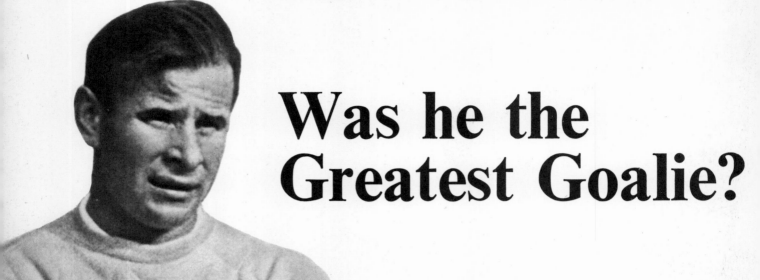

Was he the Greatest Goalie?

When the 1966 World Cup Finals ended at Wembley the individual honours were awarded. Among them was the medal for the best goalkeeper. It went to the Russian giant Lev Yashin and his selection received universal approval. Not only had he earned the highest praise for his superb goalkeeping but the big man from Moscow gained the respect and admiration of both players and fans for his geniality and sportsmanship.

Born in 1929 Lev Yashin played basketball until the age of 17 but took to football with his works team and in 1949 joined Moscow Dynamo. He quickly developed under the coaching guidance of that brilliant Russian goalkeeping genius Tiger Khomich and when the master retired in 1953 the pupil took over. Since then he has played in nearly 400 games for Dynamo and appeared 100 times for Soviet Union sides, including three World Cups — 1958, 1962 and 1966. He has also been selected for several Rest of the World teams. Now a senior physical training instructor in Moscow he decided last season to ''retire'' from football, but has since proved that he is still indispensable to Moscow Dynamo and to his country. One thing is certain, the football world will never forget Lev Yashin, the genial giant who made goalkeeping look so easy.

FERREIRA DA SILVA EUSEBIO

Surely the greatest player in Europe. A genius with a football and scorer of fantastic goals. There are few superlatives that could not be coupled with the name Eusebio. Born in Mozambique of poor parents, he played his early football barefooted in the dusty streets. He was taken from the local Sporting Club of Lourenço Marques to join Benfica in 1960 and in less than 12 months was making his international debut for Portugal.

From then on his career has been one of the most romantic in the game's history. "The Black Pearl" has found fame and fortune in football, but more than this, he has earned the respect and admiration of all Europe for his whole-hearted and modest approach to the game he loves and plays so well.

PETER OSGOOD

Tall, good-looking idol of the Chelsea supporters, has had a meteoric rise to fame. Born at Windsor he was playing with a Sunday morning team when Chelsea invited him for a trial. He was then only 16. Within a year he was in the first team at centre-forward and earning rave Press notices. A broken leg delayed his progress but in 1967–68 season he soared back to stardom and gained the first of his international honours in the Under-23 side.

Elegant in style, almost arrogant in his supreme self-confidence, scorer of fantastic goals, Peter Osgood has become an outstanding personality in English football — and certainly one of the most dynamic strikers.

MARIO COLUNA

Captain of Benfica; capped many times for Portugal at inside-forward and wing-half; a really magnificent footballer in every way and a very fine sportsman. A native of Mozambique, aged 33, he has played in five European Cup Finals and skippered the Benfica side in the memorable 1968 Wembley Final against Bobby Charlton's heroes of Manchester United. He also captained Portugal in the 1966 World Cup games. In his younger days, Coluna was a fine athlete, specialising in the long jump. He joined Benfica from Deportivo F.C. as a centre-forward.

IAM McFAUL

Iam is one of the smallest goalies in the First Division — only 5 ft. 9½ in. in height — but he's also one of the most dependable 'keepers in the country. Swiftly agile, with lightning reflexes and a high degree of courage, skill and self-confidence. He comes from Coleraine and played his earlier football with Linfield, the famous Irish League club, with whom he gained his first international cap, against England in 1966. Two months later he was transferred to Newcastle United as understudy to Gordon Marshall. During the next two seasons he made only 11 appearances in the League side, but at the start of the 1968–69 season was given his big chance. His fine performances between the posts was one of the reasons why Newcastle United reached the Final of the European Fairs Cup — and went on to beat Hungary's Ujpest Doza in two sensational matches to take the trophy. In this dramatic picture Iam McFaul proves his incredible leaping ability as he punches the ball away from Chelsea's John Dempsey (blue shirt) in a First Division game.

NEWCASTLE UNITED

Hail to the 1969 European Fairs Cup winners:

Left to right: (*back row*) Ollie Burton, Alan Foggon, Dave Smith (Coach), Frank Clark, Eric Ross;
(*centre row*) John McNamee, John Craggs, John Hope, Iam McFaul, Tommy Gibb, Wyn Davies;
(*front row*) Jim Scott, Jackie Sinclair,
Bob Moncur (Captain), Manager Joe Harvey, Bryan "Pop" Robson, David Craig, Ben Arentoft.

The Magpies of Tyneside were
the second British club to win the Fairs Cup since its introduction in 1958.
Leeds United held it in 1968 and Arsenal last season.

Manchester United's little Irishman has been described as "the most exciting footballer of this generation". The Soccer writers have used every superlative in the English language to eulogise the tiny "boy from Belfast" who is now the biggest crowd-puller in British football. He has been called a showman — a big-head because of his "gamesmanship" — but George Best is a young man with a personality of his own and a super-abundance of self-confidence. He is a character idolised by fans not only at Old Trafford. Controversial maybe, but above all else he is a brilliant footballer, a match-winner who, in spite of other outside interests, puts the game first and foremost in his life.

GEORGE BEST

DENIS LAW

A truly "Great Scot". Brilliant individualist and scorer of fantastic goals, he is one of the outstanding personalities of modern Soccer. Born at Aberdeen he joined Huddersfield Town as a boy; developed into a star; was transferred to Manchester City for £55,000 (March 1960) but 15 months later moved to Torino (Italy) for a fee of £100,000.

A year later he returned to Manchester to don United's colours for a fee of £116,000. Since then he has won League Championship and F.A. Cup honours but missed the greatest moment in United's history, the European Cup triumph, through injury. He has also played in more than 40 games for Scotland.

JOHN HOLSGROVE

This 6 ft. 2½ in., massively built centre-half is a real power in the Wolves defensive system.
Born in South London he was signed as a junior amateur by both Arsenal and Spurs, but neither club offered him the big chance. He signed for Crystal Palace, first as an amateur. After only one season as a professional, Wolves paid a fee of £18,000 for the promising 18-year-old half-back. That was in May 1965. Two years later he was a member of Wolves promotion-winning team and now, after five seasons with the club is nearing his 200th League game.

GEOFF HURST

will always be remembered as the first and only player to score a hat-trick of goals in a World Cup Final. But who could ever forget his incredible performance against West Germany at Wembley in 1966?

Born at Ashton-under-Lyne he joined West Ham as a junior wing-half but switched to inside-forward. It was a switch to fame. Yet his selection as England's centre-forward a few months before the World Cup came as a surprise, but Hurst proved himself the man for the onerous job. Since then he has gone from strength to strength.

TERRY COOPER

Tough little Yorkshireman, who comes from Pontefract. Leeds United took him on to their apprentice staff in 1960 as a left-winger, but turned him into one of the most exciting, adventurous full-backs in Division 1. He loves nothing better than to join in the attack in front of goal. It was thanks to his attacking enthusiasm that Leeds United won the Football League Cup in 1968, for it was left-back Terry Cooper who scored the only goal against Arsenal at Wembley. He was also one of the team's heroes in the two-leg triumph against Ferencvaros in the Final of the 1968 Inter-Cities Fairs Cup. He gained his first England cap in March 1969 and quickly established himself as a member of the World Cup squad.

NORTHERN IRELAND

Right to left: (*back row*)
Team Manager Billy Bingham,
Martin Harvey (Sunderland),
Jimmy Nicholson (Huddersfield),

David Clements (Coventry),
Pat Jennings (Spurs),
Terry Neill (Hull City),
McFarland (Crusaders),

Derek Dougan (Wolves),
Alex Elder (Stoke),
David Craig (Newcastle),
Sam Todd (Burnley),

McGregor (Trainer);
(*front row*)
Willie Irvine (Preston),
O'Doherty (Coleraine),

Tom Jackson (Everton),
Alex McMordie (Middlesbrough),
George Best (Manchester United).

57

GEOFF STRONG

One of the most valuable players ever signed by Liverpool. He joined the Anfield club as a forward but has since proved his all-round ability as a utility player. In the 1968–69 season he settled down as a fast, resourceful full-back, but his best position is that of an attacking wing-half. He joined Arsenal in 1958 as an inexperienced youngster from West Stanley, Co. Durham, and quickly developed as a scoring inside-forward. He moved to Liverpool in November 1964 for a fee of £40,000 and in May 1965 won a Cup medal when he stepped into the Final team as deputy for injured right-half Gordon Milne.

"WE'VE WON IT!"

"We've won it!" Skipper Tony Book proudly parades the F.A. Cup after Manchester City's victory over Leicester at Wembley in April 1969. Tony, joint "Footballer of the Year for 1969", rides on the shoulders of young Tommy Booth, with Francis Lee (*left*) and Harry Dowd.

WOLFGANG WEBER

The world will always remember Wolfgang Weber as the man who scored the sensational last-minute equalising goal at Wembley in the 1966 World Cup Final — the goal that forced extra time to be played. England won the trophy but no man fought harder for West Germany than the rugged, tireless Wolfgang, who has been one of the finest defensive "cover-men" in European football for several years.

A star of the Cologne club and many times West German international, he was only 21 years of age when he scored that history-making goal in the World Cup Final.

BRIAN KIDD/TOMMY BOOTH

Two of the bright young men who have helped to put Manchester on top of the football world.

Brian Kidd, born and reared in Manchester, entered the big-time arena soon after the start of the 1967—68 season and ended it with a European Cup medal and England Under-23 caps. Today the tall young inside-forward is an established member of Manchester United Present and a star of Manchester United Future.

The rise to stardom of Tommy Booth with Manchester City is very similar to the Brian Kidd saga. Tall, 19-year-old Tommy, Mancunian to his roots, was hurled into the maelstrom of First Division football in October 1968. He took his chance so well that he became City's regular centre-half and six months after his remarkable debut was chosen for England's Under-23 team. Strong, confident, cool and resolute under pressure, Tommy Booth could be the natural successor to Jackie Charlton and Brian Labone.

DUNDEE UNITED

Players in the group are:
left to right: (*back row*) Andy Rolland, Jimmy Briggs, Dennis Gillespie, Donald Mackay,
Alec Reid, Doug Smith (Captain), Alec Stuart;
(*front row*) Jim Cameron, Dave Hogg, Alan Gordon, Kenny Cameron, Ian Mitchell, Ian Scott, Stewart Markland.

For many years after their entry into the Scottish League
in 1923, Dundee United wore black and white, but in 1969
the "Tannadice Terrors" became the "Tannadice Tangerines"
when they changed their colours.

ALAN HODGKINSON

One of the smallest goalkeepers in League football, but
one of the best. Alan joined Sheffield United about
15 years ago, after a short spell with Worksop Town.
Since the 1956–57 season he has played in well over
600 games for United and has been rewarded with
Under-23 and senior caps for England.
A charming personality and a fine sportsman in every
way, Alan Hodgkinson has proved that height is not an
essential to success as a goalkeeper. He has achieved
fame with his studious approach to his job and the
development of lightning-quick reflexes.

INTERNATIONAL CAPTAINS

Two of the greatest half-backs in British football take the field as leaders of their country's crack teams — Mike England (Wales) and Bobby Moore (England). Both made their first appearance in international football in the 1961—62 season and their combined total of caps is well over 100. Bobby Moore has spent all his football career with West Ham United, while Mike England, born in North Wales, began his Soccer life with Blackburn Rovers before moving to the Spurs in August 1966 for a fee of £95,000.

Both he and Bobby Moore rank among the elite of British Soccer stars, for each is not only superbly proficient in his own particular sphere of the game, but both have the flair for leadership.

JOHN RADFORD

Arsenal's tall, long-striding wing-striker took his first strides into First Division football in 1964. He has now appeared in nearly 200 League games and scored over 60 goals, many of them as the result of his remarkable aptitude for running into goal-shooting position.

A Yorkshireman from Hemsworth he was playing with a local youth club when offered an apprenticeship at Highbury. In the 1968–69 season he not only topped the Arsenal score list with 15 goals but gained England Under-23 caps and a senior outing against Rumania at Wembley. He was not an outstanding success in that match but other chances must come, for John Radford, a big favourite at Highbury, is one of the most exciting wing-raiders in the First Division, a man capable of winning a game with one flash of his own inspiring brilliance.

DICK KRZYWICKI

In spite of his name Dick was born at Penley, Flintshire, of Polish parents. He grew up at Leek, Staffordshire, and attracted the attention of several Midlands clubs with his fine football in local schools teams. West Bromwich Albion signed him as an apprentice in 1963 and he made his League debut in December 1964 at the age of 16, several months before he signed pro. forms. Since then he has made encouraging progress as winger or inside-forward. Last season he joined Huddersfield Town for a £45,000 fee and gained Welsh International honours.

TOMMY WRIGHT

One of Everton's "home-made" stars. Tommy was born in Merseyside, played for the local schools team and joined the Goodison staff as an apprentice at the age of 15. In those days he was a promising inside-forward, but the Everton coaches switched him to full-back — and to stardom. He made his League debut in 1964, aged 19, and quickly settled down as partner to Ray Wilson. He won a Cup medal in 1966 when Everton beat Sheffield Wednesday in a sensational Final and was on the losing side at Wembley two years later. He gained his first England Under-23 honour in 1967 and was promoted to Sir Alf Ramsey's senior side against Russia in 1968. He is now one of the finest right-backs in the game, but his best years are still ahead of him.

COLIN STEIN

In October 1968 Rangers secured Colin's transfer from Hibernian for a fee of £100,000. It was the first ever six-figure deal between Scottish clubs. The clever 21-year-old centre-forward proved his value when, in his first match for Rangers, against Arbroath, he scored a hat-trick in four minutes and followed this astonishing feat with three more goals in the next game.

He made his debut for Hibernian in the 1965–66 season, became an outstanding scorer and in season 1967–68 hit 26 League and Cup goals. He gained Under-23 selection for Scotland. Everton immediately sought his transfer but he preferred to remain in Scotland and join Rangers.

In May 1969 he was given his chance as Scotland's centre-forward in the Home International Championship games and continued his goalscoring triumphs of his first appearances for Scotland earlier that season when he cracked in six goals in the two World Cup games with Cyprus.

It is interesting to recall that when young Colin Stein played for junior club Armadale Thistle he was — a right-back! Then in a match against a Hibernian team he was switched to centre-forward. He scored twice and was immediately signed by Hibs for a fee of £200. Three years later his transfer value had risen to £100,000.

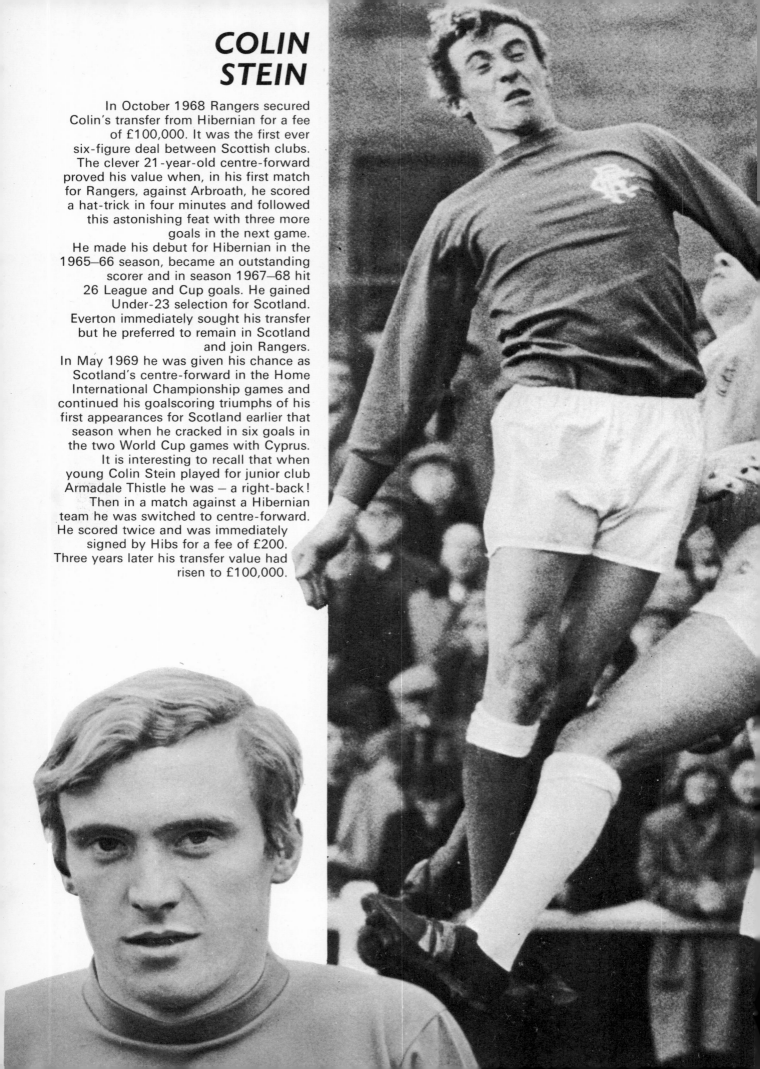

WILLIE CARLIN

"Wee Willie" — for he stands only 5 ft. 4 in. — has to rely on immaculate ball control and highly developed positional sense in his role as a midfield schemer. A native of Liverpool, he was the star of England's schoolboys sides in 1956 and a member of the Liverpool Boys' team that won the English Schools Trophy. He joined the Anfield club as a junior but was allowed to leave for Halifax Town. There he began to reveal his potential: moved on to Carlisle United, and in 1967 to Sheffield United.

In September 1968 Derby County, seeking a midfield "general" to help Skipper Dave Mackay, chose Willie Carlin and willingly paid Sheffield United a fee of £60,000 — nearly £1,000 an inch!

MIKE BAILEY

captain of the Wolves, was a wee forward playing in Suffolk schools football when Charlton Athletic invited him to join their junior staff. He blossomed into stardom as a wing-half and in 1965 gained his first England cap, after skippering the Under-23 side. That same season he was transferred to Wolves, and it was his inspiring captaincy and dynamic enthusiasm that helped to put his club back into the First Division in 1967.

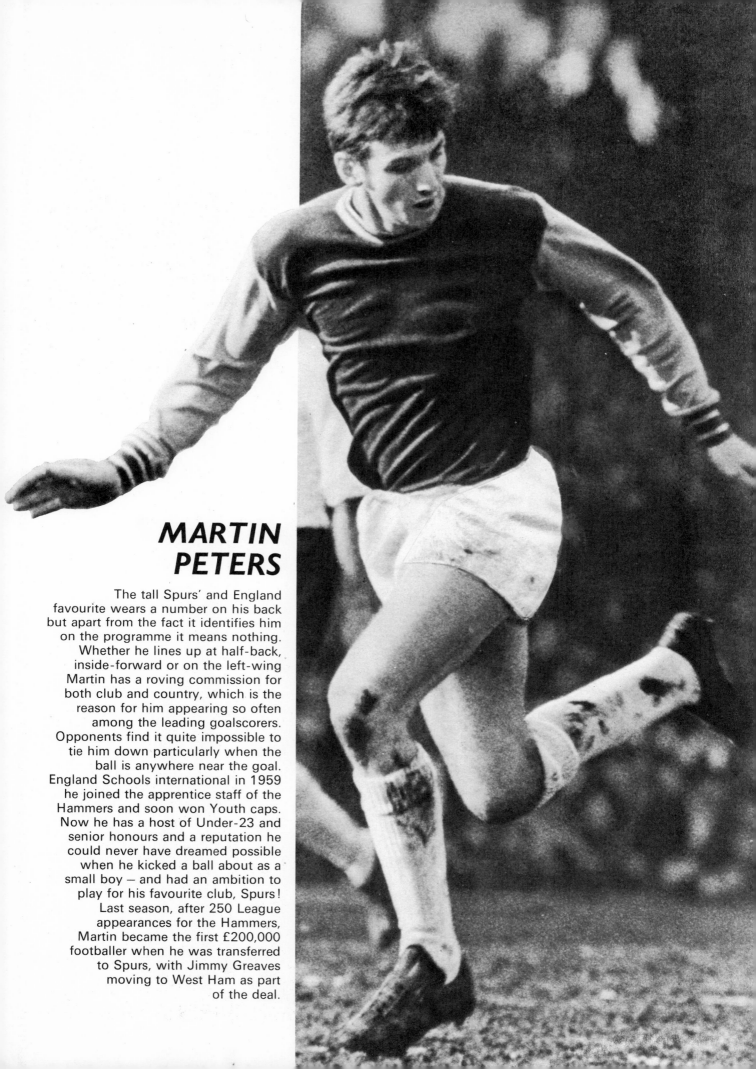

MARTIN PETERS

The tall Spurs' and England favourite wears a number on his back but apart from the fact it identifies him on the programme it means nothing. Whether he lines up at half-back, inside-forward or on the left-wing Martin has a roving commission for both club and country, which is the reason for him appearing so often among the leading goalscorers. Opponents find it quite impossible to tie him down particularly when the ball is anywhere near the goal. England Schools international in 1959 he joined the apprentice staff of the Hammers and soon won Youth caps. Now he has a host of Under-23 and senior honours and a reputation he could never have dreamed possible when he kicked a ball about as a small boy — and had an ambition to play for his favourite club, Spurs! Last season, after 250 League appearances for the Hammers, Martin became the first £200,000 footballer when he was transferred to Spurs, with Jimmy Greaves moving to West Ham as part of the deal.

JOHN LOUGHLAN

When Crystal Palace signed this stocky young full-back from Scottish club Morton in September 1968 for a fee of £15,000 Manager Bert Head completed the transfer of a player he had watched for several months previously. Although practically unknown to London fans when he arrived at Selhurst the Scot quickly earned the acclaim of the club's supporters, and became a tower of strength in the battle for promotion to the First Division. Born at Coatbridge he earned considerable success at school, where his team-mates included Celtic's giant John Hughes and Danny Hegan, now with Wolves. Leaving school with Soccer aspirations he joined Leicester City as an apprentice. After three years at Filbert Street, and very few opportunities to gain top-class experience, John Loughlan returned home to try his luck with Morton. Now he has made such progress that international honours may not be so very far away.

He smiled his way to Soccer Success

When Manchester City won the Cup at Wembley in 1969 they completed a wonderful honours hat-trick — Division 2 Champions 1966; League Champions 1968 and F.A. Cup winners 1969. The man who led City, the club that had languished in the shadow of their neighbours, United's "Red Devils", to fame and glory was their manager Joe Mercer — the man with the biggest smile in Soccer. Few men have achieved more in the football world or shown greater fortitude than Joe Mercer, from Ellesmere Port, Cheshire. He joined Everton at the age of 16, earned £5 a week when he wore the Goodison club's colours for the first time in 1935 and became one of the finest left-half-backs in the game. He gained five England caps — it might have been many more but for the war when he appeared in 22 unofficial internationals; and won Cup and League Championship medals with Everton. Then, at the age of 31, after 15 years at Goodison, he moved to Arsenal for a £7,000 fee (imagine it!) and began a second career. Joe's bandy legs and inspiring example worked wonders at Highbury and he skippered the Gunners to two League Championships, one Cup Final triumph and one Wembley defeat. Then, eight years after joining Arsenal, at the age of 39, a broken leg brought his amazing career to an end.

Joe returned to the family grocery business on Merseyside — but not for long. Soccer was in his blood and he became a manager, first with Sheffield United and then with Aston Villa. Life wasn't easy, for Joe Mercer never spared himself, but his health broke and he was forced to give up on doctor's orders. We all felt this was the end of Joe Mercer as a manager, but his indefatigable enthusiasm could not be suppressed. In 1965 he was persuaded to take over the managerial chair at Maine Road. Success was immediate and today the man who has twice overcome misfortune and enforced "retirement" is again enjoying the smile of fortune. No one has earned it more than Joe Mercer, whose team last season won the Football League Cup and the European Cup-winners' trophy.

Joe Mercer as captain of Arsenal.

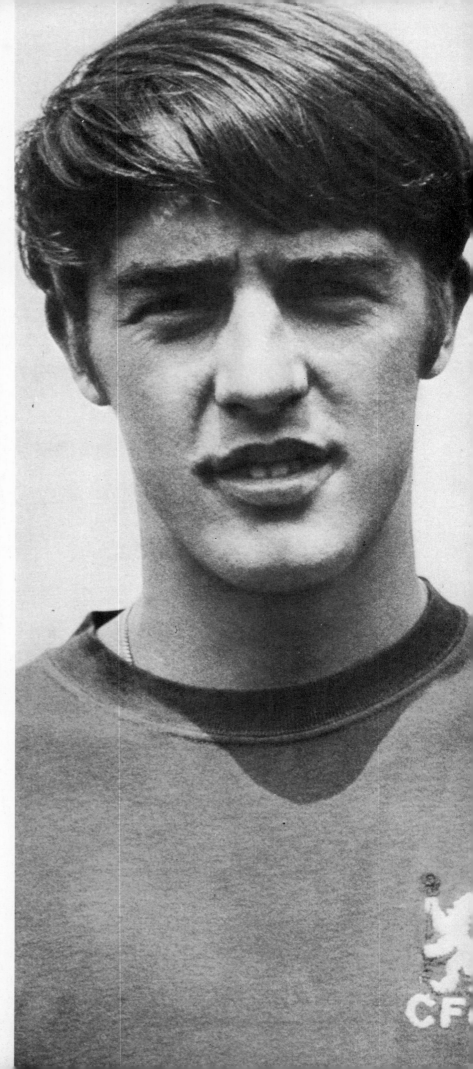

IAN HUTCHINSON

Chelsea's tall, well-built young striker was practically unknown before the 1968–69 season, but he flashed into the limelight and developed with meteoric speed. Born in Derby he played for Burton Albion before joining Cambridge United in the Southern League. Then news reached Chelsea from one of their scouts sent to watch a Southern League goalkeeper that he had spotted a centre-forward "star of the future" named Hutchinson. Chelsea acted on this tip and last July secured the tall youngster's transfer for a fee of £2,500 — which was to be doubled if he played in ten League games. The extra fee had to be paid for Ian gained his chance in the Stamford Bridge side and displayed amazing maturity for a player with such a dearth of big-time experience. Only 21, there seems a big future for this dashing, fearless goalscorer, who is also a long throw-in specialist. Before becoming a full-time professional footballer he completed a five-year apprenticeship as a millwright.

BRIAN CLARK

Hefty inside-forward and goalgetter of Cardiff City and a great favourite with the Ninian Park fans. A native of Bristol he grew up in a football home, for his father was at one time the very popular leading goalscorer for Bristol City. Brian followed in Dad's footer-steps and joined Bristol City as a boy. He made his first League appearance in 1962 and became a menacing scorer with 83 goals in 194 games for City. In 1966 he moved on to Huddersfield Town, but in February 1968 was transferred to Cardiff City where he linked up with Welsh international John Toshack to form a very dangerous double spearhead.

JOHN ROBSON

Youngest member of Derby County's brilliant Second Division Championship side in 1969 but the short, slim 18 year-old full-back showed amazing maturity and confidence considering his age and limited first-class experience. Durham born, John was playing at wing-half for Birtley Community Centre, a local junior club, when Manager Brian Clough offered him a trial with Derby County. Towards the end of the 1967–68 season he made his first appearance in the League side and proved his potential.

The following season under the inspiring leadership of the veteran Scot Dave Mackay, John Robson developed into a star-class left-back and his success augurs well for a very bright future.

HUGH McILMOYLE

The tall Scot from Port Glasgow has travelled around more than a bit since he left the Cambuslang club in 1960 to try his Soccer luck with Leicester City. A year later he was City's surprise choice for centre-forward in the Cup Final against Tottenham Hotspur.

Since then "Mac" has worn the colours of Rotherham United; Carlisle, for whom he scored 39 League goals in season 1963–64; Wolves, who paid £30,000 for his transfer in October 1964; and Bristol City, when a fee of £27,000 changed hands in March 1967. But in 1968 he returned to Carlisle United where he had done so well during his previous "residence". Last September, however, he was allowed to move to Middlesbrough, for a £55,000 fee. Goalscorers are worth their weight in gold!

CHARLIE WRIGHT

Charlton Athletic's big Scottish goalkeeper joined the club in March 1966 from Grimsby Town and after a slow start has become one of the safest 'keepers in Division 2. A native of Glasgow he spent a short spell with Rangers but failed to make much of an impression. Next he played for Workington Town before moving to Grimsby and to Charlton. He is now a fully qualified F.A. coach and is proving of great assistance in developing the younger members of the Charlton Athletic staff.

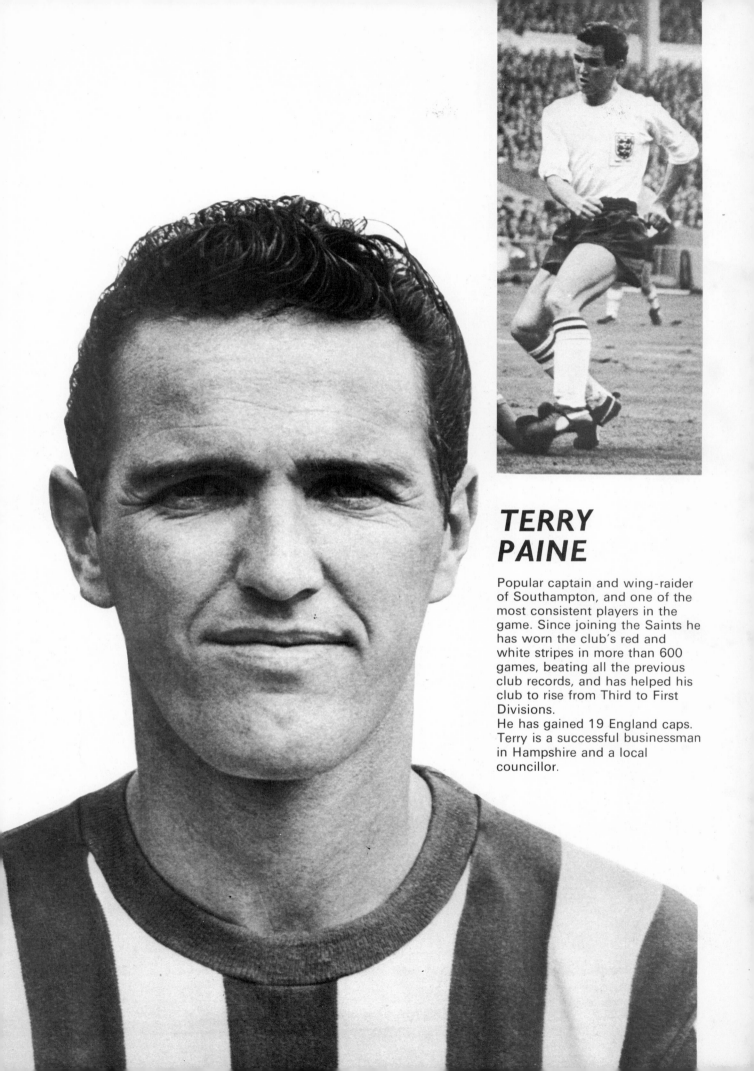

TERRY PAINE

Popular captain and wing-raider of Southampton, and one of the most consistent players in the game. Since joining the Saints he has worn the club's red and white stripes in more than 600 games, beating all the previous club records, and has helped his club to rise from Third to First Divisions.

He has gained 19 England caps. Terry is a successful businessman in Hampshire and a local councillor.

Beau Georgie Best

No player of modern times has received greater acclaim than George Best. Managers, players, fans and Soccer scribes all over Europe are unanimous in agreement that the little Irishman is a genius with a football. But there is more to George Best's fantastic popularity than his ability to play football of incredible brilliance. His name has become a byword among modern teenagers. He has created an image and developed a personality akin to that of the leading pop idols. He was one of the first footballers to adopt the longish hair style and was immediately dubbed "Beatle Best".

It caught the fans' fancy — even though some "old-timers" were inclined to be critical. Today, seven years after he left his Belfast home, a wee boy of 15, George Best has achieved fame — and fortune both on the football field and in the business world. This son of a Belfast shipyard worker has proved that he has a very fertile brain as well as fabulous feet and has capitalised on his popularity. Who can blame him?

He enjoys an occasional game of cricket and here he is taking the field to open the batting for Manchester United.

A man of many interests, George Best must be one of the busiest of all Soccer stars. He runs two successful boutiques in Manchester, one in partnership with Mike Summerbee, the Manchester City and England forward. You can be sure that these two boutiques are the mecca of the modern-minded boys and girls for miles around. In Manchester it is the ambition of all "with it" youngsters to be "dressed by Best."
But that is not the extent of George's business interests. His name is in great demand in Press and advertising both as star footballer and as expert in modern fashion. But in spite of all his "outside". interests and the excessive demands on his time, George Best has never neglected his training or his own physical fitness. Football is his profession. He is wise enough to realise that football has been — and will continue to be — his finest publicity agent in his business life.

George is also in great demand as a model for the makers and distributors of the most modern young men's clothes, which he himself wears so naturally, as these two pictures prove. He really is an amazing young man. Genius on the football field and trend-setter in the world of fashion.

JOHNNY GILES

Brilliant little midfield general of Leeds United and one of the greatest inside-forwards in modern football. A native of Dublin he came to the fore as a tiny right-winger with the Home Park club and joined Manchester United in November 1957. Republic of Ireland international honours followed and in 1963 he won a Cup medal with United. But before the start of the following season Johnny had been transferred to Leeds United for a fee of £32,000. Now he has passed the 200 mark in League appearances alone for the Elland Roaders and has been one of the "senior architects" in the team's climb to the realms of Soccer glory. He switched from the wing to inside-forward when the wee Scot Bobby Collins left Leeds after skippering them to the 1965 Cup Final.

No player has worked harder to achieve Cup and Championship successes, for he and his captain, Billy Bremner, have developed an uncanny partnership both in defence and attack.

JOE ROYLE

One of Everton's many home-bred products he joined the Goodison Park brigade straight from school as a promising right-half, after skippering the Lancashire Schools team. In 1965, before he had reached the professional age of 17, he was given his League baptism — at centre-forward. Today the tall, weighty young Liverpudlian is one of England's brightest strikers. In May 1968 he was awarded his England Under-23 cap to add to the Youth honour he won before he had joined the ranks of the stars. The future looks rosy for Royle.

JIM PEARCE

At the opening of the 1968–69 season Jim Pearce was just "a promising reserve" with Tottenham Hotspur as a goalscoring utility forward. Then came the serious injury to £125,000 Martin Chivers. Spurs were faced with a dilemma. A big-money replacement for the tall goalscorer seemed to be essential.

But they found the man for the job in young Jimmy Pearce. He stepped into the team and gained high praise for his enthusiasm and tenacity. He's a local lad and a born Spurs' fan. England capped him as a schoolboy in 1963 and he straightway joined Spurs as an apprentice. He's a lad to watch for the future.

ALAN GILZEAN

Once a regular centre-forward the big, powerful Scot is now a valuable utility striker, ready to give of his best in whichever attack position he is chosen. Alan comes from Perth and was playing as a junior with Coupar Angus when Dundee took him on to their staff. He developed into a very fine centre-forward and leading goalscorer in the side that won the Scottish League Championship in 1962. In December 1964 he was transferred to the Spurs for £72,500 and has more than repaid that fee. He helped the Tottenham team to victory in the 1967 Cup Final with Chelsea and has won 20 Scottish international caps.

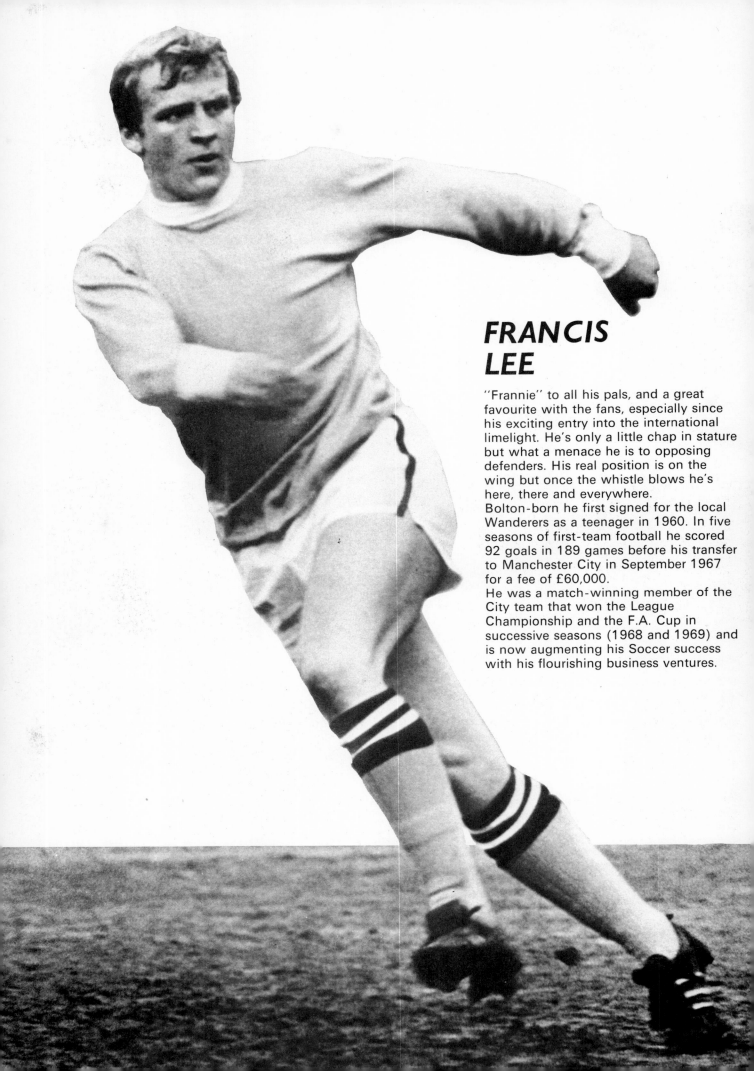

FRANCIS LEE

''Frannie'' to all his pals, and a great favourite with the fans, especially since his exciting entry into the international limelight. He's only a little chap in stature but what a menace he is to opposing defenders. His real position is on the wing but once the whistle blows he's here, there and everywhere.

Bolton-born he first signed for the local Wanderers as a teenager in 1960. In five seasons of first-team football he scored 92 goals in 189 games before his transfer to Manchester City in September 1967 for a fee of £60,000.

He was a match-winning member of the City team that won the League Championship and the F.A. Cup in successive seasons (1968 and 1969) and is now augmenting his Soccer success with his flourishing business ventures.

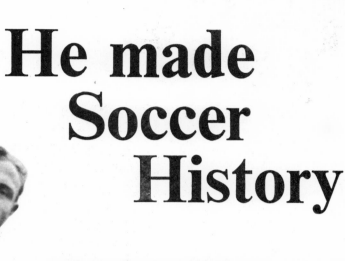

He made Soccer History

from Ground Staff Boy to International "Centurion"

On 28 September 1946 a stocky, fair-haired young right-half from Wolverhampton Wanderers made his debut for England against Ireland. On 11 April 1959 that same player captained England against Scotland at Wembley and became the first player in the history of the game to complete a century of appearances for his country. He added five more caps and then called it a day. But the name of Billy Wright will never be erased from the Soccer records. He joined the Wolves in 1938 as a wee, shy 15-year-old schoolboy from his native Ironbridge, in Shropshire, to work on the ground staff. After the war he became the club captain and made a dramatic appearance in the England side. Year after year he maintained his position in the international side, taking over the captaincy in 1948 and in 1954 switching his position to centre-half in

the World Cup side. His 100 appearances for England covered 26 different countries and three World Cup competitions. During that century of internationals he was on the losing side on only 18 occasions, a truly remarkable record.

These historic pictures show Billy Wright leading out the England side for his 100th international against Scotland, led by Bobby Evans, of Celtic, at Wembley in April 1959, and the joyous scene at the end of this memorable game. England beat the Scots 1–0 and Billy was carried shoulder high from the field by his colleagues Ron Clayton (left), of Blackburn Rovers, and Don Howe, of West Bromwich Albion.

Today Billy Wright is a producer of sports programmes on commercial television in the Midlands, after a short spell as manager of Arsenal.

WYN DAVIES

Few countries have a finer trio of strikers than Wales with those brilliant six-footers John Toshack (Cardiff City), Ron Davies (Southampton) and Wyn Davies (Newcastle United) acting as a three-pronged spearhead. Not the least of these is Wyn Davies, dominating centre-forward in his own right and a real menace in front of goal with his heading skill. A native of Caernarvon he stepped on to the senior Soccer stage with Wrexham in 1960 and quickly earned a reputation as a powerful leader and goalscorer. Bolton Wanderers made a bargain capture in March 1962 when they signed Wyn for £20,000 and soon saw him gain his first senior caps for Wales, to add to his Youth and Under-23 honours. His final move to Newcastle United came in October 1966 when a fee of £80,000 changed hands. Wyn is not such a prolific goalgetter as his namesake Ron, but his fellow attackers of Newcastle pay high tribute to his unstinting efforts as a maker of chances for their sharpshooting. His many Welsh caps are proof of his value to his country.

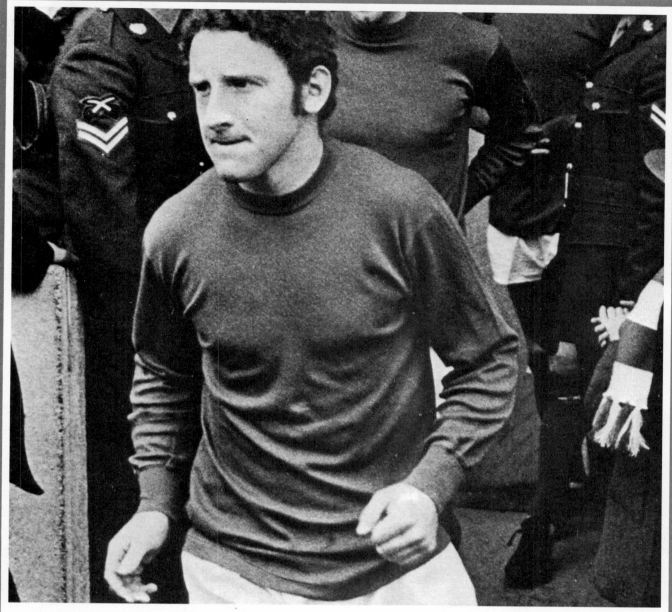

CARLO SARTORI

One of the brightest of Manchester United's stars of the future, for although his chances so far have been limited, the tiny lad has impressed everyone at Old Trafford with his mature football brain and the undoubted skills of the natural inside-forward. Yet he might never have made the grade. Born at Calderzone, Italy, his parents settled in Manchester when he was still a baby. Carlo soon became crazy on football and by the age of 15 had made a big impression with Manchester Schools teams. He applied for an apprenticeship with Manchester United, but after a trial the wee lad with the flaming head of hair was told that he was too small and frail. As a consolation he was signed on as an amateur.

Two years later he had made such progress that he was offered a full professional engagement. Carlo, known as Harpo to his team-mates, was reared in the Collyhurst district of Manchester — from whence came Nobby Stiles and Brian Kidd. He could — and should — become the third United star from that Manchester area. Carlo is no longer the puny youngster of a few years ago. His mother's cooking has had much to do with his build-up, and in this "at home" picture Carlo is enjoying his favourite meal, chicken cacciatore, prepared by Signora Pia Sartori.

Bobby Charlton
SOCCER GENTLEMAN

MAN OF HONOUR
PLAYER WITHOUT AN ENEMY

In 1969 Bobby Charlton received the O.B.E. for his service to football. After the investiture at Buckingham Palace he is pictured with his wife Norma and daughters Suzanne (left) and Andrea.

1958 – "New boy" Bobby Charlton (left) welcomed by England captain Billy Wright before his first "cap" against Scotland. The other player is Jim Langley (Fulham).

1969 – Bobby has lost some of his hair but none of his flair. The "new boy" of 1958 has become the "veteran" of the England side – the experienced general.

"There is nothing unusual about me except that having been born among footballers I was gifted with a natural talent for the game . . . I live for football."

That was written ten years ago by the man who is now known all over the football world as one of the greatest sportsmen ever to grace the game – Bobby Charlton. Throughout his years as a topline player the quiet, modest Manchester United star has never ceased to thrill the millions who watch him from the stands and terraces of the big grounds and on the TV screen with his immaculate artistry and those bombshell shots that leave goalies gasping. But Bobby will always be remembered for his dedication and devotion to all the finer moral standards of true sportsmanship.

It truly can be said of the "boy from Ashington, Northumberland" that he has never made an enemy on the football field – or off it.

From the day in 1953 when he made his first appearance at Wembley as a member of an England Schools team and received glowing Press praise for his two-goal display, to that memorable May day in 1968 when he stepped up to the Wembley Royal Box to receive the European Cup, he has achieved every honour in the game – but fame and success have never changed the Bobby Charlton outlook. He is Soccer's gentleman, respected by opponents, admired by referees and an idol with fans everywhere. Of course he is proud of all the honours he has won – F.A. Cup medal, two League Championship medals and the European Cup with Manchester United; a World Cup-winner's medal (1966), when he was Footballer of the Year both in this country and in Europe – but you'll never hear Bobby boasting about his achievements. He leaves that to others. So long as he can continue to give of his best on the field, knowing that he is giving enjoyment to the fans, he is happy.

(Picture left) Gentleman Bobby receives the Footballer of the Year Trophy (1966).

UWE
SEELER

greatest of all West German centre-forwards, gained his first international cap against England in 1954 at the age of 17. Twelve years later he captained his country in the World Cup Final at Wembley and proved that age had not dimmed his wonderful skill and enthusiasm. Last season he talked of retirement but was restored to the West German side for the Mexican World Cup tournament. He joined the Hamburg S.V. club as a small boy and rose to fame in their colours. His father and brother also played for Hamburg.

KARL HEINZ
SCHNELLINGER

tall, blond West German full-back, is such a great footballer that he could play well in any position. His first club was Duren (his birthplace); he gained his first cap in 1958 when only 19 and playing for Cologne, but all his finest years have been spent in Italy with Roma, Mantova and Milan. He played for the Rest of the World XI against England in 1963 and in the 1966 World Cup Final.

. . . Jolly old Pals . . .

One of the lighter sides of First Division football was captured by a cameraman when Bobby Moore, the West Ham skipper, and Jimmy Greaves, then Spurs' master marksman, were in direct opposition. Just a few months later these two great players became club colleagues when Jimmy was transferred to the Hammers as part of the Martin Peters deal. It was a happy reunion. Both were born within a bus ride of the West Ham ground and although Jimmy preferred to join Chelsea as a 15-year-old, he and Bobby first met on the football field in Youth games. In the years that followed they not only renewed their rivalry in First Division games but were members of many England Under-23 and full international sides. Their early friendship has remained throughout their years of Soccer glory and now extends into the world of business, for Bobby and Jimmy are "jolly good pals" off as well as on the field.

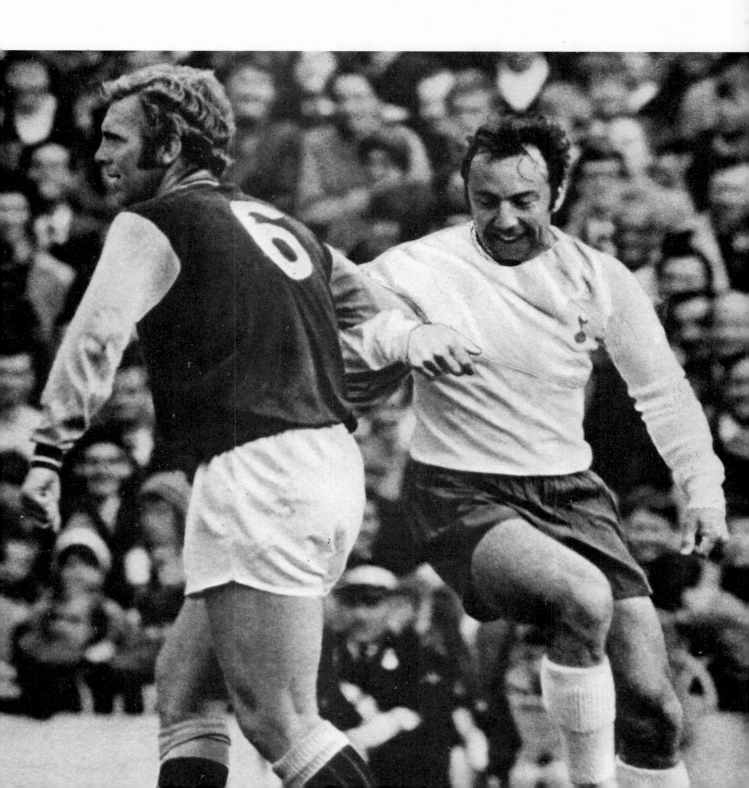

No one will ever forget the brilliance of
Gordon Banks during England's memorable
World Cup triumphs in 1966. Without a
peer as a goalkeeper he makes saving goals
look easy because of his wonderful
anticipation and lightning reactions.
Sheffield born and a superbly fit six-footer,
Gordon began his career with Chesterfield,
won his first England cap in 1963 with
Leicester City and was transferred to Stoke
City in 1967 for a fee exceeding £50,000.
He has played more times for England than
any other goalkeeper in history.

GORDON BANKS